DENYING ONE'S SELF
IN
A SELFISH WORLD

By James Puckett

Reasons to Deny One's Self

Copyright © 2005 by James E. Puckett

ISBN 0-7414-2610-2

Scriptures quotations are from the Kings James Version of the Bible by Thomas Nelson 1990

Published by:

INFINITY
PUBLISHING.COM

1094 New DeHaven Street, Suite 100
West Conshohocken, PA 19428-2713
Info@buybooksontheweb.com
www.buybooksontheweb.com
Toll-free (877) BUY BOOK
Local Phone (610) 941-9999
Fax (610) 941-9959

∞

Printed in the United States of America

Printed on Recycled Paper

Published June 2005

Table of Contents

Acknowledgments

My special thanks to Laura Freeman for her consultation and editorial work in the preparation of this manuscript. Thank you Laura for being a friend and such a blessing to me.

And to my wife, Brenda, who have supported me all these years of writing. Thanks Brenda for your love and support. Thank you for all your prayers while I worked so hard to complete this book.

INTRODUCTION

Dear Reader,

I want to share with you the inspired Word of God on the subject of your *self*. People get in trouble over their selves every day. Both Christians and Non-Christians have the problem of not controlling their selves. Self will make decisions both big and small for your life that you will have to live with for the rest of your life. People everyday miss the plan and purpose that God has for their lives because of their selves. I believe that before any Christian can serve and worship God in spirit and in truth and do great things for God, they must first remove one's self from the picture. Step back from personal desires, and look at what needs to be done.

The Random House College Dictionary gives this definition of self. Self is a person's nature, character, and personal interest. Self can also be defined as an individual character or behavior. Self is just a metaphor for the word flesh. Without your flesh, self wouldn't have anything to make demands upon. Self is in operation when your flesh wants to do something that goes against the Word of God. Every Christian should have a goal to follow Christ.

Every Christian should strive to be a disciplined person. The only way one can be a disciplined follower of Christ is to deny one's self. To do this Jesus said that you must deny yourself. We must set our personal agendas aside and follow the agendas that God has for our lives. The world and the society in which we live in have many people focusing on themselves. That's why it's important that we as a people demand that our leaders uphold and support healthy and moral biblical standards. In this book I expose some problems with self, and with the help of the Holy Spirit, share some insights on why Christians must deny their selves.

James E. Puckett
April 2005

CHAPTER ONE

Self Will Not Obey God

Self will keep you out of the will of God. Every time that God wants you to do something for Him, you can just about count on your self getting in the way. The old fleshly nature will rise up in you to the point where you make all sort of excuses why you can't do whatever it is that God is calling or leading you to do. Because we were created by God and for God, He wants nothing more then for us to be in His will. When I first began to write, I wasn't sure if that was God's will for me. My first book was a struggle for me to write and complete. I would ask myself, "If this is the will of God that I write this book, then why am I having such a struggle doing it"? The problem wasn't hearing God when He spoke to me. The problem was obeying God when He was speaking. God doesn't always speak to us when it's convenient or the time is just right for us. God will speak to you and I whenever He chooses. And most of the time it's not when we want to hear from Him, or when we least expect to hear from Him. Whenever or wherever He chooses to speak to us, it's up to us to obey.

The problem I faced writing my first book, and still face today, is the problem of my selfish nature. God would wake me up at all times during the night hours. I would lie in bed for hours reciting what God wanted me to write down. I tried reasoning with God. Telling Him that I had to get up in a few hours, and that I would write it down after I had woken. That didn't work. I tried writing from my bed while still laying down. That didn't work. My self wouldn't allow my flesh to get out of bed. After making every excuse that I could think of, which God didn't honor, I would get out of bed. After this went on for some time, I began to accept the call and realize that this was the will of God for my life. I had to obey God and get up, and write down the things He was telling me. I wasn't able to go back to sleep until I did just that. I couldn't put my mind on something else. All I had in my thoughts were the things that God wanted me to write down. Once I denied myself, and put myself in the position where God could really speak to me, I started to write my first book. Sometimes God would speak for five minutes, fifteen minutes, or even for as long as an hour or more. At that point it didn't matter how long God would keep me up. What mattered was that I was now in control of myself and in the will of God. I still struggle with myself today in this area. But I have learned after my third book that this is the will of God for my life, and I have to obey to remain in His will.

I shared with you in my previous book how I wanted to do some ministry at a local detention center a few years ago. My wife and I had just arrived in Knoxville from Okinawa, Japan. I had a desire to do something worthwhile for God. Since I

2

had done this type of ministry before, I pursued it with all my heart. But I soon found out that just because I had a desire this desire was not promised to me. The desire that I had came from my head and not from God. Yes, it was a good desire, but not the will of God for my life at that time. The Scripture says, *"Delight thyself also in the Lord; and he shall give thee the desires of thine heart"(Psalm 37:4).* This doesn't means that God is going to grant every desire that you and I have. I believe that sometimes we can desire the wrong things even if we are serving the Lord with all our heart. We may think that something is right for us, but it could be all wrong if the desire is not from God. I believe that if God put the desire in our heart and spirit it will come to pass if we follow after it. It's the desire that God gives that comes from your heart. If the desire is not from God, it's from your flesh. As hard as I worked to do inmate ministry it did not materialize. There was always something preventing me from stepping off into this area of ministry. Even though it was good work, God had another job for me. Jesus even commanded us to visit those that are in prison *(Matthew 25:35-46)*, so I knew what I wanted to do. Finally I let go of my own desire and allowed room in my spirit for the Lord to give me His desire. I began to let the Spirit of God have complete control over my will. That's when He led me to the nursing home, where I ministered for over two years. Ministering at a nursing home never became a personal desire, but it did fulfill my desire to do ministry.

3

"Among whom also we all had our conversation in times past in the lusts of our flesh, fulfilling the desires of the flesh and of the mind; and were by nature the children of wrath, even as others."

(Ephesians 2:3)

There are Christians today that are out of the will of God because of this very issue. Christians must deal with the issue of themselves. It may not be God's will that you write a book or minister to the elderly in a nursing home. Whatever God's will be for your life, you will not walk in accordance with Him until you deal with yourself. When you revolve your life around your own self you are your own god.

<u>NOTES</u>

CHAPTER TWO

Self Will Not Follow Christ

Before any Christian can expect to follow Christ as His disciple, they must deny themselves. Following Christ as His disciple is no easy task. Jesus wants you to forsake all.

> *"Then said Jesus unto his disciples, If any man will come after me, let him deny himself, and take up his cross, and follow me.*
>
> *For whosoever will save his life shall lose it: and whosoever will lose his life for my sake shall find it.*
>
> *For what is a man profited, if he shall gain the whole world, and lose his own soul? Or what shall a man give in exchange for his soul"?*
>
> *(Matthew 16:24-26)*

Jesus is saying here that if you as a disciple plan to follow Him, you must put first things first. And the first thing is to deal with and deny *yourself.* We must put self aside and put Christ in His place. Being a disciple of Jesus simply means being His disciplined follower. To follow Jesus is to let His thoughts become our thoughts and His ways become our ways. Jesus is so serious about this issue that He even asks us as Christians to forsake the ones who are close to us.

> *"And Jesus said unto them, Verily I say unto you, That ye which have followed me, in the regeneration when the Son of man shall sit in the throne of glory, ye also shall sit upon twelve thrones, judging the twelve tribes of Israel.*
>
> *And every one that hath forsaken houses, or brethren, or sisters, or father, or mother, or wife, or children, or land, for my name's sake, shall receive an hundredfold, and shall inherit everlasting life.*
>
> *But many that are first shall be last; and the last shall be first."*
>
> *(Matthew 19:28-30)*

These are very strong statements that Jesus made to His disciples. Jesus knew that in order for His disciples to follow Him and do the things that He asked them to do, they first had to deny themselves of the things that would be a hindrance to their new lives. Jesus did not tell the disciples to forsake their families, just not to put them before Him. In other words, nothing or anyone should come between them and Jesus.

I believe there will be many Christians who will be surprised on judgment day. There are many Christians who stand out in their community, church, or even around the world, but they haven't given up all for Christ. Maybe something is stopping you from being all you could be for Christ. You refuse to let go of parts of your life for selfish reasons. You may be worried about what a family member is going to say, worried that your spouse is going to leave you - it could be a number of things. This is your self now working on the flesh. Then there are those who are always working behind the scenes. Some may not respect your new life. For example, your own sister or brother will not speak to you, or have anything to do with you because you chose Christ over them. You are the Christians who might be the first to receive your rewards.

Christians must set aside their agendas and focus on the kingdom of God in order to follow Christ. This means that self must be put in check whenever need be. In the book of Matthew, chapter 26, beginning at verse 31, we read where Jesus is telling His disciples that all of them will go against Him for their own sake. But look at the discussion Peter and Jesus are having.

"But after I am risen again, I will go before you into Galilee.

Peter answered and said unto him, though all men shall be offended because of thee, yet will I never be offended.

Jesus said unto him, Verily I say unto thee, that this night, before the cock crow, thou shalt deny me thrice.

Peter said unto him, Though I should die with thee, yet will I not deny thee. Likewise also said all the disciples."

(Matthew 26:32-35)

I believe that Peter decided to speak up before any of the other disciples did because possibly he didn't trust them. Peter could have been trying to prove that he was more committed than the other disciples were. What Peter didn't know was that he couldn't even trust himself. He never considered himself getting in the way of following Christ. Many of us are like that today. We make all sorts of promises and commitments while things are cool and no action is required of us. But as soon as things begin to heat up, we develop a problem with our selves. Sometimes we tend to talk a good game, but when it's time to play we refuse to get into the action. Peter was so sure of himself not to deny Jesus. It even sounded so good to the other disciples that they all agreed with him. I believe Jesus corrected Peter because He knew Peter wouldn't be able to live up to his promise because of his selfishness. Jesus stopped him dead in his tracks and told Peter that he would deny his Lord over himself. Twice Peter denied even being with Jesus *(Matthew 26:69-72)*. The Bible says the second time he denied with an oath. The third time he denied even knowing Jesus. The Bible says Peter became so angry that he began to curse and swear *(Matthew 26:73-74)*. Then Jesus' words came true, and the cock crowed.

Peter could not follow Christ because of his selfish flesh. The Bible says that Peter went out and wept bitterly *(Matthew 26:75)*. Peter had all good intentions to do the right thing. But when it came down to acknowledging and following Jesus or saving himself, he chose self.

Following Christ also means being a faithful servant. It doesn't matter if we are serving in a public or private place; our goal should be to serve faithfully. To be faithful, a servant must be unselfish and consistent in his duties *(Ephesians 4:1)*. One of these duties includes getting to work on time and performing your assigned duties as unto the Lord. I believe it is disrespectful to your supervisor and co-workers for you to continue to show-up late to your job day after day. I wonder how quickly we could correct ourselves if our employer informed us that we had to start clocking in and out every day and we would be only paid for the time we worked? Most of us would probably straighten up pretty fast. No one is going to wait on you or I to show up at our jobs for work to be done. If we can get to work on time we should without hesitation get to church on time. If you are serving in an area of helps ministry, your help is needed. People are counting on you and expect for you to be there on time, at a certain place. If you are just at church to hear the preaching then you should be in the sanctuary at a respectful time, and seated waiting on the service to start. I believe it is disrespectful for people to crowd the sanctuary after the service has started. Most of the time these people are somewhere in the building, doing something other than making their way to the place where they need to be. The praise leader is not going to wait on you to move inside the sanctuary before he or she leads the people into praise and worship. The pastor is not going to wait on you to take your seat at the table before he serves the food. Walking in after service has started is a selfish way of saying, "I don't respect what is about to take place." If we don't respect the house of God, we are not faithful in our service to Him.

NOTES

CHAPTER THREE

One's Self Will Not Love Christ

Some Christians love themselves more than they love Christ. I am not suggesting that you shouldn't love yourself. The Bible commands Christians to love their neighbor as they love themselves. So loving our neighbors is equal to loving ourselves. You must first love yourself before that love can be extended to your neighbor. This type of love is placed in a person's heart once they are saved. *"And hope maketh not ashamed; because the love of God is shed abroad in our hearts by the Holy Ghost which is given unto us"* *(Romans 5:5)*. It is God's will that we as Christians love one another with the same love His Son showed on Calvary's cross. But if you love yourself to the point where Christ is not first in your life, then you love yourself more than you love Christ.

You can't possibly love your brother if you don't love Christ. If you don't love Christ or your brother or sister, then who is it that you love? It is yourself that you have love for more than anything else. Jesus said many times throughout the New Testament, *"If ye love me, keep my commandments"* *(John 14:15)*. We can make all sorts of excuses for our selfishness and wrongdoings, but when we get right down to it, it's because we love ourselves more than we love Christ. Why do Christians continue to struggle with sin in their lives? All they have to do is make the choice to change. I am not suggesting that Christians don't want to change or make an attempt to change, but what I am saying is that when Christians try to change, they have to deal with their fleshly nature, which is one's self. We must first look in the mirror and see ourselves for who we really are. We can change our outer makeup, but only God can change our inner makeup. This can only be done with the help of the Holy Spirit and the Word of God. That is why it is so important that we do as the Word of God tells us to do.

> *"For if any man be a hearer of the Word, and not a doer, he is like unto a man beholding his natural face in a glass:*
>
> *For he beholdeth himself, and goeth his way, and straightway forgetteth what manner of man he was."*
>
> *(James 1:23-24)*

Self will always want things to remain the same. Remember self feeds off the flesh. If you try to change the things that your flesh is accustomed to, conflict begins. So in order to satisfy your flesh, you allow yourself to remain as you are. The self-nature will always be challenging for Christians. The only way I believe you and I can control self and bring it under subjection is to choose to walk in the love of God. This is easier said than done. Some people are considered impossible to love. This is true if we don't love God like we should. How should we love God?

> *"And He answering said, Thou shalt Love the Lord thy God with all thy heart, and with all thy soul, and with all thy strength, and with all thy mind; and thy neighbour as thyself.*
>
> *And He said unto him, Thou hast answered right: this do, and thou shalt live."*
>
> *(Luke 10:27-28)*

Everything we do in life should be centered on loving Christ. Loving that person you thought you could never love again is possible when you love Christ first. In 1 Corinthians, chapter 13, Paul lists what charity (love) is, and what it is not. In I Corinthians 13:4-8, Paul lets us know that we may be capable of doing lots of things, but if we don't walk in love, we profit nothing. Selfishness and love cannot be in operation at the same time. Love is selfless. We must first love Christ if we are to love others.

> *"Beloved, let us love one another: for love is of God; and every one that*

loveth is born of God, and knowteh God.

He that loveth not knoweth not God; God is love."

(1 John 4:8-9)

One's self cannot be involved in this process. How can we love Christ when we are stuck on ourselves? How can we say we love Christ when we are centered on ourselves? We may say we love Christ, but if we are focused on ourselves, it is self that we truly love. When we love material things and ourselves too much, we love God less. We must learn to rule our own spirit from selfishness *(Proverbs 16:32).*

By practicing selfishness, our relationships with others become stronger. When we love Christ more than we love ourselves, we won't get offended easily. Love covers a multitude of sins *(1 Peter 4:8).* We can accept others' faults, and learn to forgive more easily. We have a debt to love one another. *"Owe no man any thing, but to love one another: for he that loveth another hath fulfilled the law" (Romans 13:8).* As we learn to walk more in love we will live less selfishly. We must always put Christ first. We stop putting Christ first when we become selfish. When God delivered the children of Israel out of their afflictions they gave themselves to Him.

"And this they did, not as we hoped, but first gave their own selves to the Lord, and unto us by the will of God."

(2 Corinthians 8:5)

Anything or anyone that we put before God is an "idol." God hates idols. Your house, car, job, spouse, friend, or your money can all be idols. Even you can be an idol to yourself. God said to keep *your selves* from idols *(I John 5:21).* We have to keep our selves from idols. Therefore you must keep you from yourself. If we love God we will not live selfishly.

> *"But if any man love God, the same is known of him.*
>
> *As concerning therefore the eating of those things that are offered in sacrifice unto idol is nothing in the world, and that there is none other God but one."*

(1 Corinthians 8:3-4)

> *"For they themselves shew of us what manner of entering in we had unto you, and how ye turned to God from idols to serve the living and true God."*

(1 Thessalonians 1:9)

We must become more God conscious and less *self* conscious.

<u>NOTES</u>

CHAPTER FOUR

Self Will Not Consider Others

Some people can be very resentful toward others. Holding grudges is no way for a Christian to live. A person who holds grudges against others is also unwilling to consider others. Feelings of dissatisfaction about what someone else has, or his or her good fortune is a selfish act.

> *"Let nothing be done through strife or vainglory; but in lowliness of mind let each esteem other better than themselves.*
>
> *Look not every man on his own things, but every man also on the things of others."*
>
> *(Philippians 2:3-4)*

Christians are commanded by God to show respect and consideration for others. It amazes me how we can claim to always put other people's needs before our own. But most of the time we are self-serving. We fail to show any compassion for others when we are operating in self. When was the last time you put someone else's needs before your own? Or should I ask when was the last time you put the need of others ahead of your *wants*? This is the problem with self. Self will almost always demand that its *wants* be fulfilled before it reaches out for the *needs* of others. When was the last time you literally put your life on hold to see about the need of someone else? Yet we say we care about how others feel, and how a situation will affect them. I am not suggesting we run to the rescue of every person that needs help. No one person can respond to every person that has a need. But there are times we are called to put others needs above our own needs. We will never understand how to do this if we are always concerned about ourselves. Too many times we are more concerned with *me, myself, and I*. We fail to honor Christ when we neglect to consider others' needs.

Have you ever considered all the pain and suffering that some people put on others? These people would rather satisfy themselves and what they love to do rather than consider the hurt and pain being put on others. Let me give you an example: A person who drives an automobile under the influence of alcohol does not consider others. This person is more concerned about satisfying his or her feeling and flesh than the safety of others. There is a law that prohibits this action but it is many times violated. People are seriously injured and some even lose their lives. These people disregard the law at the expense of satisfying themselves. These people don't obey the law, nor do they consider the life of others.

Why do some people say they were born gay or homosexual? I believe it's because they refuse to take a good look at themselves as they relate to their creator. All they can think about is satisfying their own flesh and desires. Choosing to carry out sin in life is done by one's own will. Why do two people of the same sex want to join together? Again, they are too prideful to look past their own desires and to see what God has already desired for them.

Believers must learn to consider others' needs before their own. The majority of believers would have to think really hard about this. This is a Bible truth that many believers fail to live up to because they are deeply into themselves. The only truth they want to comply with is the truth that will satisfy their needs at the given moment. This selfish truth that they are bowing down to is a false truth that is from the pit of hell. It is a truth that will change with the environment or the circumstances. It is a truth based on how they feel at the present time. This is not an absolute truth. Only God's Word is the absolute truth, and we must submit to Him in any situation. This could be through our employer, parents, law enforcement, spiritual leaders, or even the doctor.

Let me give you another example. Let's say I have some symptoms of some type of sickness or illness. I need to be seen by a medical doctor. I go to the doctor and tell him my problem and what hurts me. At this point I have submitted my health and well-being into the hands of the doctor. I no longer get to decide what is best for my health. The doctor recommends a prescription drug or some other method of treatment. He tells me I must comply with his instructions or the problem could get worse. I am having a hard time obeying the doctor's orders.

I continue in my ways and the problem gets worse. Who am I pleasing? If you answered "myself", you are right. Who am I hurting? I am hurting myself, my wife, my children, my friends and family, and I am hurting God by not obeying the doctor's orders, and for not considering the pain and hurt of others. This is selfish and could have a lifetime of pain and suffering attached to it. To tell you the truth, when you made Jesus Christ the Lord of your life, you made Him Lord of all. That includes everything pertaining to your life. You no longer have your own life to do as you please with it. He tells you what to do, when to do it, and how long to do it. Is Jesus the Lord of your life, or do you just claim Him as Savior? Look for ways today to put others needs and concerns before your own, and then do the right thing.

Some people have a challenge in taking care of their bodies. Some face more of a challenge than others do. Why do some people continue to smoke cigarettes when they know it is harmful to their health? Why do some people continue to drink alcohol when the doctor has told them that if they don't stop it will kill them? Some people work hard at maintaining their bodies. Some people work hard at destroying their bodies. But a good, spiritual Christian would never confess to this. If you are a Christian, then your body doesn't belong to you. And to add to that, if you are married and are a Christian, you now have to share your body with two elements – the Holy Spirit, and your spouse. You may be saying, "This is my body and I can treat it any way I choose!"

> *"Know ye not that ye are the temple of God, and that the Spirit of God dwelleth in you?*
>
> *If any man defile the temple of God, him shall God destroy; for the temple of God is holy, which temple ye are."*
>
> *(1Corinthians 3:16-17)*

If you are a Christian your body belongs to God. It is the place that God has chosen for His Spirit to live. You may have total control over your body when it comes to making choices for it, but the choices you make will not only affect you as a person, it will affect the God in your life. If you destroy your body the Spirit of God has nowhere to live. Being selfish and thinking that you can just do whatever you please with your body is to deny the Spirit of God the right to dwell there. When the Spirit feels He is no longer welcome, He begins to move out. When this happens, decay of the body sets in.

People ask me all the time, "Why do you exercise and eat like you do?" "Why do you get up so early in the morning and exercise?" My answer is always, "Because I like it, and it makes me feel good." But this is only partial truth. My sole reason for doing what I do five days a week is because I am not only living for myself, but I have a wife, three children, two grandchildren, a father, and three sisters. I have people in my life that count on me and I count on them. My supervisor where I work is counting on me to report to work everyday and be ready to do what I was hired to do. My co-workers are counting on me to support, to help, to love, to encourage, and to lead. I am counting on them to do the same. My church family is counting on me to be where I have committed myself. I am counting on them to do the same. There are certain members in our church that look to me for support and encouragement. I am expected to love, to help, and to lead. Because I love and care about them, I don't want to put any undue hardship on any of them because of my selfishness. That is why I work so hard to maintain my health.

> *"The wife hath not power of her own body, but the husband: and likewise also the husband hath not power of his own body, but the wife."*
>
> *(1 Corinthians 7:4)*

The application of this passage of Scripture was written in the context of a husband and wife being intimate with one another. But I believe that in a spousal relationship, consideration should be taken on how each person cares for his or her physical body. Remember if I chose to treat my body any old way, it will not only affect just my body and my spirit, but it will also affect my spouse. If I don't consider how I care for my body physically and spiritually, my body will decay and eventually will no longer be able to function properly. When my body stops functioning, I stop functioning in life. When this happens someone else who is physically capable is required to step in and lend a hand. In marriage this is normally the husband or wife. I need my wife, and she needs me. And it's important that I tell her this. And it's important that I hear this from her. My desire is to live a long, healthy, prosperous, life with my wife. And when we are satisfied on this earth we will go home to be with the Lord. I believe it is disrespectful to God and to your spouse if you don't take care of your body.

Relationships require a special kind of unselfishness. A married relationship requires mutual unselfishness. You don't know how selfish you really are until you get married. You were accustomed to doing things that required only your decision. Now you have to share those things with someone else. Many marriages end in divorce because one person refuses to consider the needs and desires of the other person. I know by now someone is saying, "I don't need anyone else but Jesus." Well, that sounds good, and we do need Jesus, but this is selfish thinking. We also need one another. God didn't make man to be alone in this world. God even created man because He wanted someone to have fellowship with. God didn't even like the idea of man not having someone that was compatible to him, so He made woman. We need each other, so learn to live each day not only for yourself, but also for the people in your life and those around you. Get rid of those bad habits of not taking care of your physical and spiritual body. Bad habits are a result of letting self have its way. The longer we let self have its way, the more self will take control.

It's easy for us to become selfish and not consider others when it comes to maintaining good physical and spiritual health. Just the other day I had a conversation with a woman who admitted she had let her selfish nature control her eating habits. This lady whom I have known for about a month now, willingly confessed to me that she had to do something about her weight. I did not initiate this conversation, she did. It was obvious that she needed to lose some weight. I am not judging her; she brought up the topic herself. Without any shame she said to me, "James, I have got to lose some weight; can you tell me what I need to eat." I was very sensitive to her question, and could see in her eyes that she was serious about wanting to lose weight. I said to her, "You may not like me any more if I tell you what you should and shouldn't be eating if you want to lose weight." We talked about foods that were healthy and foods that were unhealthy. She was listening to every thing that I told her, but began to show just how selfish she was as I suggested the foods that she should stay away from and the foods she should make part of her diet. I told her how important I thought exercising was to overall weight loss. I noticed that she did not show the same enthusiasm and commitment as she did at the beginning of our conversation. Self had begun to step in and dominate her will.

She told me how tired she gets just from walking a short distance. She admitted that her health was declining fast. I asked her if she had someone close to her that would hold her accountable for what she ate and how she exercised. She told me no. I suggested her eleven-year-old daughter. After all they live in the same house. Then I told her how I really felt. I told her if she knew that she needed to lose weight and didn't put effort toward it, she was being selfish and not thinking about her daughter, but only thinking about herself. I asked her would she like to see her daughter grow up, finish high school, go on to college, maybe get married one day and have children. She answered yes. Then I asked her would she like to see her grandchildren grow up. She answered yes. I told her that in order to better her chances of seeing these things come to pass, she would need to do what she knows she needs to do about her health problem – start exercising and eating right.

I explained to her that it would take discipline and perseverance on her part. When we have allowed self to control our lives for most of our life, it will take a strong will on our part to make positive changes.

Our conversation ended with that said. Whether she will bring her flesh and selfish will under her subjection is her decision. God has given us all free will to do with our bodies whatever we choose. Even though He has told us how we should maintain and take care of our bodies, He will not force us to do these things. We cannot even try until we choose to deal with self. If we don't challenge our flesh it will continue to control our life. If this woman wants to see changes in her health, she has got to change her habits. Right now she has the habit of letting herself control how she looks, feels, and lives. We have heard the saying, "If we want different results, we can't keep doing the same thing."

Because this woman chose to continue to do the same thing, it resulted in more of the same results - a worsened state of physical and spiritual health. And the only way to starts reversing this is to begin dealing with self. I am in no way suggesting that you get up five days a week before daylight to run and lift weights. But we as Christians should be able to find some time out of our busy schedule to minister to God by exercising the body and maintaining it in such a way that will glorify Him. I believe we all can do this if we choose to not focus totally on ourselves, but also consider the people that God has placed in our lives.

In my previous book I shared with you how I had to stay focused when I was going through Warrant Officer School. I was doing this to reach a personal goal. This was a dream of mine from early in my military career. But I learned early that the key to survival was not working alone, but working as a team. Survival was based on teamwork and helping other members in my class when help was needed. This was something that the entire class quickly learned. The people that tried to do it alone quickly learned that the system did not operate that way, and paid for their selfishness. God has a system too. His system is for Christians to consider others in their time of need, and this requires that they set aside their own agenda for a period of time if need be. This is something Christians really have to work on, because self doesn't care anything about others and doesn't care anything about what belongs to others. No matter what type of relationship you are in, in order for it to be successful, you must always consider the needs of others first.

In my book *Keeping Your Mind Renewed In Your Spiritual Walk With Christ* I shared how several of my co-workers took me to this all female restaurant to eat. They all knew I was a Christian and I made it very clear that I didn't want to go there. They were not concerned about me and how I felt. They were only concerned about satisfying the *will* of their flesh.

The Bible commands Christians to pray for one another *(James 5:16)*. Most Christians would properly confess to doing this in a corporate prayer setting. But what about in your own private prayer time? How often do we pray for others and their needs without mentioning our list to God? Most of the times we are only concerned about our selves. Little do we know that when we pray for others and their needs, our prayers are answered. We are told to seek the kingdom of God and His righteousness first and not our selves *(Matthew 6:33)*.

<u>NOTES</u>

CHAPTER FIVE

Self Will Not Forgive

Some people are so indulgent of themselves that they won't forgive others or won't accept forgiveness from others. It is hard for them to say, "I am sorry, I was wrong." Not forgiving or not wanting to forgive can be defined as selfish pride. This is an area that we all struggle with, both Christian and non-Christian. Have you ever said something or did something to hurt someone? Has someone ever hurt your feelings so badly that you confessed never to have anything else to do with him or her no matter if they were Christian or not? Even if it was one hundred percent justified in what you did or said, Christians do not have the option to deny someone forgiveness. Maybe you were right, but you are wrong in not forgiving them. Maybe they were right, but you are still wrong in not forgiving them. I believe many times Christians miss out on what God has planned for them simply because they refuse to forgive others. The people who choose to forgive not only give the other person a chance to recover, but it also releases the bondage and guilt that the person has placed on his own life. By not walking in forgiveness, we invite the enemy into our lives. Sometimes we are trying to determine where the enemy is coming from that is attacking us when the enemy is within ourselves.

By granting another person forgiveness, you will be better able to receive God's blessings. I was talking with another member of our church about how blessed we are to have a church like our, and pastors who teach and preach the Word of God. She was telling me how the message the night before had blessed her. She said she began to ask God why she couldn't seem to get a breakthrough in her finances. She said she paid her tithes, she attended church regularly, she served in the church, she treated people right, and she loved God with all her heart. She said the next day God revealed to her that she still had some unforgiveness in her heart towards another person, and she had to go to that person and make things right. She was so excited because she knew this was the one thing that was holding her back from God's blessings. There have been many testimonies in our church about how God revealed to them that they needed to go to grant someone forgiveness.

Jesus Himself taught His disciples that forgiving others was vital in their walk with Him and their relationship to the Father.

> *"For if ye forgive men their trespasses, your heavenly Father will also forgive you:*
>
> *But if ye forgive not men their trespasses, neither will your Father forgive your trespasses."*
>
> (Matthew 6:14-15)

Imagine, our heavenly Father holding a grudge against His children! No, I don't believe that's what the above verses mean. The passage is saying that God the Father cannot forgive an unforgiving heart. Forgiving others is a matter of condition and will. We must find the will to forgive. Jesus told Peter he was to forgive four hundred and ninety times a day if need be.

> *"Then came Peter to Him, and said, Lord, how oft shall my brother sin against me, and I forgive him? Till seven times?*
>
> *Jesus saith unto him, I say not unto thee, until seven times: but, until seventy times seven."*
>
> *(Matthew 18:21-22)*

I would have to admit that I have been around people who would push this number to the limit. The point is, we are not to spend our day counting how many times we forgive a person, but we are to forgive whenever forgiveness is needed.

"I will forgive, but I won't forget." Ever heard those words before? Maybe you were the one saying them. What is really being said is, "I forgive you at the present time, but if you cross me again, if you push that button again, I will bring up the past." This is not what the Bible teaches. I will admit it is hard to forget when someone has done you wrong. I believe that we all remember the good as well as the bad things that people do to us, or that we have done to other people. But there is no reason to bring it up again if it has already been dealt with. It seems that all to often people choose to cease communication with each other when someone gets hurt rather than working at reconciliation. The hurt is still there and when we see that person, or someone brings up his or her name, we began to reminisce on the past. Christians have a power living inside of them to forgive and forget *(1 John 4:4)*. He is called the Holy Spirit. The Holy Spirit is capable of removing hate, jealousy, faultfinding, and anything else that will have your flesh feeding off, but only if you allow Him to. Non-Christians don't have this power so they love to bring up the past of someone's wrongdoing. Because they have no other example to follow after, they follow the devil's example. The devil loves to satisfy oneself. One way he does this is by bringing up people past failures. That's why he is called the "accuser of our brethren" *(Revelation 12:10)*. Once an issue is settled, it should be forgotten and never brought up again, but self is a master at recalling one's past failures.

A while back I got a phone call from a family member I have not heard from in a while. The last time we talked over the phone the conversation was heated, which is a nice way of describing it. This person blamed me for most of the things that went wrong in his life. I wanted to and tried hard to have a relationship with him, but he wouldn't allow it. I would always explain to him why it was important to let go of any resentment or strife over what had happened in the past. Over the years, every time we tried to talk about things we always ended on a bitter note. For more than fifteen years he kept this bitterness and unforgiveness inside him. During this fifteen year period there was no real relationship between the two of us.

The day I got the call I was glad to hear from him. Just the tone in his voice made me feel good. I knew right away that it was a good call. All the bad feelings that he had kept locked inside him over the fifteen years as it related to me, he released himself from it that day. He talked and I listened. Tears came to my eyes as he talked. He forgave me, and asked for my forgiveness for the way he treated me all these years. He told me that he accepts the life that I have made for myself, and wanted to learn from me and not criticize what I am doing with my life. He told me that he had come to a point where all the negativity inside him was literally killing him and ruining his life. He went on to say that he was calling and going to everyone that he had done wrong to. He said he felt better and his life was already getting better. After he was done saying what he had to say, I thanked him and told him that I accepted his forgiveness. I told him that I have been praying for this day since 1989. His reply was "I guess it worked." I told him, "Yes, prayer works."

I had already forgiven him and made my peace with God about eleven years ago. Now God has made it possible for us to make peace with each other. Our relationship with each other is getting better with each passing day. According to the Bible each person has to confess their own sins to be forgiven and cleansed of their sins *(1 John 1:9)*. This has to be done by the will of one's self. When we choose not to forgive, we are choosing not to be forgiven and cleansed by our Heavenly Father.

When God sent His Son Jesus to the cross to die in our place, He was forgiving man and forgetting all the sins of man. When Jesus said, *"Father, into thy hands I commend my spirit"(Luke 23:46)*, He was forgiving the Father and forgetting the things that were done to Him on the way to Calvary and at Calvary. Jesus even asked the Father to forgive the men who would cast lots for His clothes *(Luke 23:34)*. If the Father forgave and forgot, if Jesus forgave and forgot, who are we to do any less? When Jesus was nailed to the cross He took all the sins of man with Him to never bring them up again *(Colossians 2:13-14)*.

> *"He will turn again, he will have compassion upon us; he will subdue out iniquities; and thou wilt cast all their sins into the depths of the sea."*
>
> *(Micah 7:9)*

> *"For I will be merciful to their unrighteousness, and their sins and their iniquities will I remember no more."*
>
> *(Hebrews 8:12)*

Other people, Christian or Non-Christian, have no right to bring up your past failures. Likewise, you have no right to bring up someone else's past failures. If we are not careful, our selfish flesh will respond and began to tell all it knows. Learn to forgive and forget.

> *"And he said to them all, If any man will come after me, let him deny himself, and take up his cross daily, and follow me."*
>
> *(Luke 9:23)*

<u>NOTES</u>

CHAPTER SIX

Self Always Has A Motive

We all have motives for the things that we do in life. Motives are things that cause or prompt a person to act a certain way or do a certain thing. Our lives are a series of choices. Each choice we make has a motive behind it. The question is, is the motive a good one, or a bad one? But if we are not careful those motives can become self-serving. The motives of most unsaved people are for their own gain and benefit. They do things, or fail to do things for selfish gain. They have no good intentions for the other person involved. Granted his or her intention may not be to hurt anyone, but most of the time someone always ends up getting hurt. Motives that truly have someone else's interest in mind are good motives even if that person doesn't think so.

God had a motive for the death of Jesus on the cross for you and I. What was God's motive for this act of love? He tells us in two verses of Scripture:

> *"For God so loved the world, that He gave His only begotten Son, that whosoever believeth in Him should not perish, but have everlasting life.*

For God sent not His Son into the world to condemn the world; but that the world through Him might be saved."

(John 3:16-17)

This was the absolute motive of God. His motive was not for man to suffer in the lake of fire. I have had unsaved people tell me that God knows that they are not saved, and if God wants them saved He will save them. Yes, God knows if you are saved or not. God is omniscient; he has complete knowledge of everything. If you are not saved it also hurts the heart of God. God is also omnipotent, meaning He has almighty and infinite authority and power; but He will not make you be saved. It is a choice that each one of us has. Whether you choose to be saved or not comes with a motive for your decision. Some Christian's motive for getting saved is to keep them out of hell, but not to serve God. Some Christians motive for getting saved is to please others. I am sure there are many other motives. But the only true motive one should have for accepting Christ is the love we have for Him and what He did and is doing. Going to heaven and not hell is just a by-product for the choice.

Why do people choose not to be saved? Why do mothers choose to stop being mothers? Why do fathers choose to stop being fathers? Why do some groups decide that their concerns are more important than the good of society? Their motives are almost always for selfish gains. They remain unsaved because they have decided to not serve God. Their motive is to live their lives as they wish, and not have anyone to tell them what to do - at least not God. Their motive is to live as the world lives and do what makes them feel good, even if it's at the expense of others. I was speaking with a young man a few years ago about salvation. He told me that he was not ready to be saved because sin was too good. He was not ready to give up what he thought was fun living. His motive for not accepting Christ was that he was not ready for someone else to tell him how he should live. He was not ready to give up his *will* for the *will* of God. God gave every man his own moral free *will.*

> *"For this is good and acceptable in the sight of God our Saviour;*
>
> *Who will have all men to be saved, and to come unto the knowledge of the truth."*

> *(1 Timothy 2:3-4)*

I have shared my faith with many people who have told me that they have thought about being saved but haven't done it yet. When I asked them why, almost every time I get the same old answer – I am not ready yet. What makes people not want to be saved? What makes sinners want to keep on sinning? I believe they know that once they give their life to Christ they are required to live a certain way. This means they can no longer do their own thing and live the way they have lived in the past. Its not the fact that they are not ready yet, the real reason is they are just too much into self to see past the world's way of living and see the way of the kingdom's. Paul said, *"For he saith, I have heard thee in a time accepted, and in the day of salvation have I succoured thee: behold, now is the accepted time: behold, now is the day of salvation" (2 Corinthians 6:2).* What is your motive for being saved or not being saved? There is no right motive for not being saved. Just admit it, it's for selfish reasons.

<u>NOTES</u>

CHAPTER SEVEN

Self Is Greedy

Greediness is one of those areas that all Christians must guard against. It is no easy task for children of God not to want an abundance of things in life. I am not suggesting that we as children of God should live our lives in lack. This would be contrary to what the Bible teaches.

The type of greediness I am referring to is desiring and having things in excess just because God said you could have it. If we are not careful, we will begin to hold on to everything that God blesses us with. We will begin to praise objects rather than God. Everything that God allows to come into our possession is not only for us to enjoy and keep. Sometimes He gives us things because that's His way of getting it to someone else who really needs it. There are two things of importance that we sometimes forget as we prosper or gain material wealth. One is that we sometimes forget who made it possible, and two, we forget about others and live in a world of our own. This is not what God intended when He blessed you with material wealth. God didn't allow you to come into the possession of all these things just for you to enjoy by yourself. God told Abraham that He would bless him, and he shall be a blessing *(Genesis 12:2)*. Anything that is in excess in your life, God wants you to share it with others. You may say, "But I worked so hard for what I have." This is where we make our first mistake. Thinking that we did it all on our own is selfish pride. God warned the children of Israel for thinking and talking that way:

"But thou shalt remember the Lord thy God: for it is He that giveth thee power to get wealth, that He may establish His covenant which He sware unto thy fathers, as it is this day."

(Deuteronomy 8:18)

I am reminded of a story in the Bible where Jesus told a parable about being greedy. In Luke chapter 12, beginning at verse 15, Jesus tells us to be aware of greediness. He warns that our life should not be based on the amount of things that we have. Jesus tells the story about a certain man who has become wealthy in his lifetime. Again, there is no problem with having abundance, but this man had developed a selfish attitude. He was missing the whole meaning of him being allowed to obtain wealth. Jesus warns us not to focus entirely on our own agenda. This man had a bad case of "I and my." All his wealth was centered on him, and he was not about to share it with anyone else. He bragged about all his riches and worldly processions. This man used the word "I" six times in bragging about his wealth. He uses the word "my" five times. This man was greedy, and into himself.

He sure didn't acknowledge God at any time in his conversation. He was selfish with all the things God had blessed him with, and he wanted more of the things that he already had. This is exactly where greediness will take you. It will take you off into a world by yourself.

This man never realized that it was God who gave him the power to get the barns, goods, and fruit that he had. There are many Christians in the church today who think just as this man did. This man didn't care about anyone else but himself. He was so greedy that he was stuck on himself. He was so focused on worldly possessions that he forgot all about God and blessing others. This man had a spirit of pride about him. The Bible says, *"Pride goeth before destruction, and an haughty spirit before a fall" (Proverbs 16:18)*. We cannot serve God with a prideful attitude and a self-fulfilling goal. If we do, we can be certain that our little world we live in will come tumbling down. Trying to get everything that you can get your hands on and leaving God out of the equation is selfish, and greedy. Riches will not last forever *(Proverbs 27:24)*.

I know of Christians who have been blessed with material possessions. They have a good home, a nice car, and a well-paid job. They attend church regularly on Sundays and the mid-week service. Then one day something happens to them. All at once they think they need a part-time job so they can earn more money. It's not a good thing when money is the driving force behind one's actions.

Over a period of time the part-time job begins to wear on their physical bodies. The devil starts speaking to them saying, "You're too tired to attend church tonight." The devil always starts small. He gets you to lie out of church during the mid-week service. After he has gotten you consistent in doing this, he will move to a larger area – Sundays. Before you realize it, you are not attending church at all or at least not as regularly as you once were. The devil's plan is to stop you altogether. Just think, the desire for more money brought all this on.

God wants His children to have everything that pertains unto life and godliness *(2 Peter 1:3)*. He promised it in His Word. When things start having us, things start to control us instead of us controlling the things. Wealth is not attained by our own self-ability, but by the power that works in us *(Ephesians3:20)*. What power do you have working in you, the power of God, or the power of greediness? If God has blessed you with abundance and you should ever feel like you are getting greedy, try this – give some of it away. Like the man in the parable, building barns for the wrong reason will cause us to get greedy and forget about God. Self will always have a "get" attitude and not a "giving" attitude. Greediness always leads to something worse – thankless. People who have a selfish attitude will always be unthankful. Not one time did the man in the parable give thanks to God. Being selfish will always have you complaining about what you don't have rather than giving thanks for what you do have.

"Giving thanks always for all things unto God and the Father in the name of our Lord Jesus Christ."

(Ephesians 5:20)

<u>NOTES</u>

CHAPTER EIGHT

Self Lives In Its Own Little World

We live in a society where breaking rules and not following orders are the norm. This world is full of covenant breakers. Why do some people choose not to follow the rules they've agreed upon? Why does the doctrine have to change because your circumstances change? Why does it always have to be your way? People that live like this are self-centered. They are thinking only of themselves.

The Webster's Ninth New Collegiate Dictionary defines self-centered as: Independent of outside forces or influence; concerned solely with one's own desires, needs, or interests. Whatever it is they want to happen must take place on their terms and timetable. They block out every one else around them. How selfish can a person be to think that everyone around them must cater to his demands all of the time?

Self-centered people are very confrontational. They will get offended if confronted about their selfishness. People who are into self don't accept being told when they are wrong. They do not accept ideas or recommendations easily. Why is this? Perhaps its because they are in fear of someone being recognized above them. Or maybe they are afraid of losing their pride. It takes faith in God to move out of your little world into the kingdom of God.

> *"For whatever is born of God over-cometh the world: and this is the victory that overcometh the world, even our faith.*
>
> *Who is he that overcometh the world, but he that believeth that Jesus is the Son of God."*
>
> *(1 John 5:4-5)*

People who are self-centered are lustful and covetous. They always want what someone else has. They love the things in their world and take pride in getting them. Because their eyes are on the things of their world, they are blind to the things of God. The Bible tells Christians to not have anything to do with the world *(1 John 2:15-16)*.

People who live in their own world love to receive and never give. Jesus said, *"It is more blessed to give than to receive" (Acts 20:35)*. Many marriage covenants are broken when either the husband or the wife wants to enjoy all the benefits of being married but refuses to participate in putting anything into the marriage. This is stealing from the marriage. This will destroy a marriage or any relationship. A selfish person does not possess the desire to please his or her mate. If this happens, the relationship is being robbed of the joy, peace, love and harmony that it requires. A person in his own world has a mindset that says, "I want to get all I can, but give nothing in return." Living in a world of your own is a selfish and dangerous way of living.

In the parable of the lost son in Luke chapter 15, we see what can happen when we choose to go alone. The son went off into his world and wasted all his substances living a selfish life (Luke 15:13). But what he found on his own was not what he had expected. He thought that his fun would last and that he would always have his friends at his side. But the point I want to make is found in the following passages of Scripture.

> *"And when he came to himself, he said, How many hired servants of my father's have bread enough and to spare, and I perish with hunger!*
>
> *I will arise and go to my father, and will say unto him, Father, I have sinned against heaven, and before thee."*
>
> *(Luke 15:17-18)*

After being in his world for a period the son realized that he was out of God's will and his father's will and was pleasing himself. He was smart enough to know that he had made a bad decision and went back home. People that are in their own world are spiritually dead. If you are wondering around in your own little world you are spiritually lost. The only way that you can come alive and find yourself is to move out of your world and into the kingdom of God's house.

NOTES

Chapter Nine

Self Is Boastful

Some people just love to boast and brag on themselves. Boasting on one's self or one's accomplishments can become self-pride. When we speak of our selves and what we have done, what we have, and what we can do to the point where it becomes excessive, we are now speaking in puffed-up selfish pride and bringing attention to our selves.

Maybe you have done many things in your lifetime. Maybe you have been blessed with material wealth. But this does not give license to rub it into the face of others. The more we boast and brag the more our flesh demands that of us. Just like the man in the parable, he boasted and bragged about all he had. Never once did he give thanks to God. That made him even speak more about what he had accomplished and made him want more of what he already had.

The Bible tells us to let someone else brag and boast on us and not ourselves.

"Boast not thyself of to morrow; for thou knowest not what a day may bring forth.

Let another man praise thee, and not thine own mouth; a stranger, and not thine own lips."

(Proverbs 27:1-2)

People who love to talk about and brag on themselves will justify it as giving their testimony. Yes, there are certainly times when we as Christians will be called upon to express to others what God has done for us. But after you have given your testimony of God's goodness, let your life that you live be your testimony. Sometimes we just talk too much about what we have, where we've been, and what we've done.

If we would do more "walking the walk" than "talking the talk", we would be less likely to boast and brag. I am not implying that we shouldn't give information about our accomplishments and ourselves when the time is appropriate. There are times when we all must share things about our lives with others, but we should be careful not to bore them with unnecessary information. Some people you can't even speak to without them telling you their life history. They use this opportunity to boast and brag on themselves. Sometimes I question if some of what they are saying is true.

If you can do it, or have done it, then it should be an expression of the way you live. And if it's an expression of your life, then others will know it because your faith will produce it.

"For I say, through the grace given unto me, to every man that is among you, not to think of himself more highly than he ought to think; but think soberly, according as God hath dealt to every man the measure of faith."

(Romans 12:3)

This should leave very little room for boasting and bragging on one's self. Boasting and bragging is selfish pride toward one's self. The Bible tells us clearly that God resists the proud, but gives grace to the humble *(James 4:6)*. Show some humility toward others and hold back the excessive talk about yourself.

Going back to the man in the parable. All the times he uses "I" and "my" were a way of boasting and bragging on himself. Imaging if you were the one having this conversation with this man. You could barely get a word in because he wouldn't stop talking about himself and his possessions. This man boasted and bragged about what he had and what he was going to do. His mind was completely on him. When we boast of ourselves, we fail to consider what tomorrow could hold.

"Whereas ye know not what shall be on the morrow. For what is your life? It is even a vapour, that appeareth for a little time, and then vanisheth away.

For that ye ought to say, If the Lord will, we shall live, and do this, or that.

But now ye rejoice in your boastings: all such rejoicing is evil.

Therefore to him that knoweth to do good, and doeth it not, to him it is sin."

(James 4:14-17)

Boasting and bragging about what we are going to do is rejoicing in evil. For Christians, it is wrong, and if we continue, it is sin. We have nothing to boast about when it relates to us. All the praise and boasting should be toward God *(Psalm 34:2).*

NOTES

CHAPTER TEN

Self Is Judgmental

*"These six things doth the Lord hate;
yea, seven are an abomination unto
him:*

*A proud look, a lying tongue, and
hands that shed innocent blood,*

*An heart that deviseth wicked imagina-
tions, feet that be swift in running to
mischief,*

*A false witness that speaketh lies, and
he that soweth discord among brethren."*

(Proverbs 6:16-19)

Do you know someone who always has
something to say about everything? These people
should take a step back and realize that we do not
live in a perfect world. Everything is not going to
go the way they think it should. Neither you nor I
are the CEO of the universe. We don't process all
the answers and we are not the repositories of all
truth. The Bible is the only source for all truth.

When we must judge another person for his
or her actions, we must do it according to the
biblical standards. It is bad practice to view a

person or a situation from the standpoint of not knowing all the facts. Some people will pass judgement on things before they have had time to prove themselves. Would a farmer plant a field of wheat one week and the next week say that the wheat was no good because he hasn't seen any wheat stalks yet? No. If he were a skilled farmer he would know that it takes weeks for this to happen. He would be cursing the labor of his hands if he judged the crop before its time. When we judge things or people before the appropriate time we are cursing them. Paul put it very plainly. He said:

> *"For I know nothing by myself; yet am I not hereby justified: but he that judgeth me is the Lord.*
>
> *Therefore judge nothing before the time, until the Lord come, who both will bring to light the hidden things of darkness, and will make manifest the counsels of the hearts: and then shall every man have praise of God."*

> *(1 Corinthians 4:4-5)*

We need to let God do the judging if it does not concern us or we are not asked to get involved. Relationships will be saved, and we won't put people's personal and private business in the streets.

Self loves to stay in other people business. A person who glorifies one's self loves to talk about other people's business. They can't wait to repeat what they heard or was told, whether they know it to be true or not. The Bible calls these people busybodies.

> *"For we hear that there are some which walk among you disorderly, working not at all, but are busybodies."*
>
> *(2 Thessalonians 3:11)*

> *"And withal they learn to be idle, wandering about from house to house; and not only idle, but tattlers also and busybodies, speaking things which they ought not."*
>
> *(1 Timothy 5:13)*

> *"But let none of you suffer as a murderer, or as a thief, or as an evildoer, or as a busybody in other men's matters."*
>
> *(1 Peter 4:15)*

Busybodies always have the juicy story or are seeking those who can provide it. They want the big story so that they can pass it on to someone else. They never stop to think if what they are saying is true or not. All they want to do is satisfy their flesh by getting the story and telling it to someone else after adding their version to it. They can never quote to others exactly what was said without adding to it the things that makes their flesh feels good. They cut people into shreds with their words. Christians must be careful not to allow people to gossip into their ears. Busybodies are looking for people who will feed off what they have - something they heard about someone. I am not suggesting that you withhold important information that could be beneficial or life threatening. If you have valuable information to pass along to others do it in a professional way, without putting in your two cents.

Some people will get a preconceived notion about certain things and will buy into it if given the chance. Dan Rather, an anchorman for CBS News must have thought this way. He falsely reported on details concerning President Bush's military record. To report something on national television where over 300 million people watch and listen each day, you would think he or someone at CBS would verify the authenticity of the story, and thoroughly investigate the nature of its source. Yet when documents were presented to them discrediting President George W. Bush and his National Guard service, they took them to be true without even checking out their origin or authenticity. The story was told without any of this taking place, at least not thoroughly. The Knoxville News Sentinel newspaper dated September 21, 2004, stated, and I quote, "Rather and Burkett were well known in National Guard circles for several years for trying to discredit Bush's military record." Dan Rather, a veteran and chief anchor for CBS News, and Bill Burkett, a retired National Guard Officer, were trying to make our President, George W. Bush, look bad for his service to our country.

I believe there were two motives here. First, the writer wanted to damage the President's creditability in any way possible, at all costs. It was an attempt to kill his character and integrity. Second, to bring honor and glory to himself and CBS for being the first to break a big story. Because Dan Rather and CBS failed to properly check out the story for its authenticity, he had to apologize to the same 300 million people he broke the story to. Because of this judgmental and selfish act, four employees at CBS News were fired from their jobs. One man's selfishness has caused many people to suffer. This is truly a fulfillment of Scripture.

> *"He made a pit, and digged it, and is fallen into the ditch which he made.*
>
> *His mischief shall return upon his own head, and his violent dealing shall come down upon his own plate."*
>
> *(Psalm 7:15-16)*

> *"An ungodly man diggeth up evil: and in his lips there is as a burning fire."*
>
> *(Proverbs 16:27)*

Whether the documents were forged or fabricated, it was wrong and selfish. This was all done to try and make the most highly profiled man in the world look bad. When we place judgment on someone before hearing all sides of the story, we have just forged and fabricated things about them that may not be true. The best way I can suggest stopping this from happening to you is to "mind your own business."

Everything happens for a reason. Sometimes it is our fault, sometimes it is someone else's fault, and sometimes it no one's fault. We must not forget that there is a devil running loose on this earth. If we are not careful we will, without knowing it, place false judgment upon that person. We do this when we don't know the real story or all the details of the situation. Most of the time we see a situation and immediately place judgement without having any more information. This is selfish and shows that we have no regard for others. We must be careful not to quickly place judgment upon anyone before all the facts are out in the open.

> *"Judge not, that ye be not judged, For with what judgment ye judge, ye shall be judged: and with what measure ye mete, it shall be measured to you again."*
>
> *(Matthew 7:1)*

One's self will form an opinion without knowing the facts. Jumping to conclusions and placing judgments on people is a dangerous thing to do. We must take our mind off ourselves and think about the person the judgment is being placed on.

Just think about all the people who place their judgment on a person because of a situation. The people that are being judged now have to defend themselves against you, the rest of the church, and the world. Always give that person the benefit of the doubt. Give him the chance to tell his side of the story before passing judgment. There are always two sides to any story when we are dealing with people's lives. And remember your life can change in the wink of an eye. You may be challenged to walk in those same shoes.

Sometimes some people are so mean and selfish that they will pass judgment on someone for something, and they are guilty of the same thing. It could be sin or just going through a trial in their life. We are quick to announce what it is, and how they arrived there. The Bible warns Christians about judging others in this manner.

> *"And beholdest thou the mote that is in thy brother's eye, but considerest not the beam that is in thine own eye?*
>
> *Or how wilt thou say to thy brother, Let me pull out the mote out of thine eye; and, behold, a beam is in thine own eye?*
>
> *Thou hypocrite, first cast out the beam out of thine own eye; and then shalt thou see clearly to cast out the mote out of thy brother's eye."*
>
> *(Matthew 7:3-5)*

Don't try to give someone else advice when you haven't experienced similar hardships. It is selfish and prideful to tell someone else how he or she should live, when you yourself are living a similar life or worse. How would you feel if someone, who has never raised a child or never had children, tried to give you parenting advice? Most parents would properly be cautious about it and wouldn't put much value on it, if any. The only real truth we have to offer is the truth of what the Bible says about raising a child. All the theories in the world you may have on child rearing don't mean a thing until you've raised a child of your own. I hate nothing more than to hear someone try to counsel or give advice to someone when they themselves have no experience or knowledge on the subject whatsoever.

I can remember when I was getting ready to publish my second book. I had several people telling me how I should go about it, and what type of publishing company I should use. These were good people but I felt that they had nothing to tell me about writing a book or publishing one since they themselves had never written or published a book. I didn't tell them how I felt because maintaining the relationship was more important. If I am going to receive any type of counsel or advice from anyone, they will have to be qualified to give it. Never let someone tell you how to do something, or give you advice on what to do when he hasn't done it himself. Why would I take advice from someone telling me how to train for a marathon when he has never run one, or much less, he isn't even a runner? We should limit our advice and counsel to the areas we are trained or experienced in, and give advice only when it is welcomed. What we think or have heard about the issue isn't worth hearing. People are looking for solid answers. People might ask your opinion of something, and if they do, then your conversation should be limited to the foundations of the Bible. Try to keep your answer limited to the question that was asked. Be very cautious and choose your words very carefully. You should only dig deeper if the Holy Spirit prompts, or if you need more details for you to answer intelligently. If we are not careful we will begin to judge the person, and this is not what was asked of us. God is the only judge of man's heart. *"To the general assembly and church of the firstborn, which are written in heaven, and to God the Judge of all, and to the spirits of just men made perfect"(Hebrews 12:23).* Don't be quick to judge, but be a witness by the words that come out of your mouth, the way you act, and how you live. Use what you hear as a point of praying for that person and you won't be so quick to judge him.

> *"A false witness shall perish: but the man that heareth speaketh constantly."*
>
> *(Proverbs 21:28)*

<u>NOTES</u>

CHAPTER ELEVEN

Self Always Wants To Be Right

Do you know people who always have to have the last word? Do you know people who know something about every subject being discussed? These people want to be right, or at least think they are right. I have learned that sometimes it's ok to let the other person be right even if you know they are wrong. I am not suggesting that you compromise your beliefs. There are times when we may have to defend the things we believe. If what is being discussed will start a conflict between you and the other person, and it will not physically harm you, it's better for your spirit not to entertain it. You don't have to agree with them. It's ok to tell them that you disagree and leave it at that.

The Bible says:

> *"Be of the same mind one toward another. Mind not high things, but condescend to me of low estate. Be not wise in your own conceits.*
>
> *Recompense to no man evil for evil. Provide things honest in the sight of all men.*

If it be possible as much as lieth in you,
live peaceably with all men. "

(Romans 12:16-18)

Some people will want you to agree with them simply because they want to be right about everything, and will get angry with you if you think otherwise. Before you lose a relationship with someone you consider a friend, keep the friendship and let him be right. Pray that the darkness will be removed from his eyes, and that God will reveal His Light to him. Just remember you yourself are not perfect. We may have power, but we don't have absolute power.

People that are absorbed in their selves always want to have the last word. They have a problem with communicating with others. They will ask you a question, and before you can give an answer they are arguing with you. They don't even wait to hear your answer. Some people won't agree with you if their life depended on it. They will argue with you and disagree that the sky is blue.

Self tends to hold its own truth and deny the truth that it is confronted with. I know people that will confess, "I know what the Bible says, but it didn't really mean that." They want to have their own interpretation of the Bible. These people will not agree with you if they will not accept the truth of God's Word. *"Sanctify them through thy truth: thy word is truth" (John 17:17).* Our responsibility is to present them with the truth and let it rest.

I was in a serious conversation by email with an editorialist from the Knoxville News Sentinel newspaper. She had written an article supporting same sex marriage. After reading the article I couldn't help but to challenge what she said. I emailed her with my views backed up by the Word of God. She would email me back and I would answer her email. This went on for about three weeks or longer. This woman was so sure of herself that she wouldn't allow God's truth to be heard. She even said in her article that she believed in God. I shared God's Word with her in every one of my emails that I wrote to her, but she still refused to accept it as the truth. Each time I would tell her that I loved her, God loves her, and that I was praying for her. This lady has believed this lie pertaining to marriage for so long that she doesn't know the truth or isn't willing to accept truth when it is presented to her. She would always twist the truth to justify herself being right. This is what many religions have done. They show a form of godliness, but deny the power thereof. This is a dangerous place to live.

"This know also, that in the last days perilous times shall come.

For men shall be lovers of their own selves, covetous, boasters, proud, blasphemers, disobedient to parents, unthankful, unholy,

*Without natural affection, trucebreak-
ers, false accusers, incontinent, fierce,
despisers of those that are good,*

*Traitors, heady, highminded, lovers of
pleasures more than lovers of God;*

*Having a form of godliness, but deny-
ing the power thereof: from such turn
away."*

(2 Timothy 3:1-5)

*"Every way of a man is right in his
own eyes: but the Lord pondereth the
hearts."*

(Proverbs 21:2)

*"Speak not in the ears of a fool: for he
will despise the wisdom of thy words."*

(Proverbs 23:9)

NOTES

CHAPTER TWELVE

Self Doesn't Want To Change

"For we know that the law is spiritual: but I am carnal, sold under sin.

For that which I do I allow not: for what I would, that do I not; but what I hate, that do I."

(Romans 7:14-15)

There are some people that just refuse to change when they know change is needed. Someone once said, "When you blame others, you give up your power to change." The Bible instructs Christians to present their bodies as a living sacrifice and not be conformed to this world, but to be transformed by the renewing of their mind *(Romans 12:1-2).* Christians should want to change and make every effort to do so. It's understandable why non-Christians refuse to change. Unfortunately some Christians don't want to change. Some of us will remain as we are because it will require that we do something different than we are accustomed to. We depend on others to do what we are supposed to be doing, all because we refuse to change. We blame others for things that happens in our lives, therefore we see no need to change.

Why do people constantly arrive to their jobs late? Why do people refuse to change their eating habits, when their lifestyle could be sending them to an early grave? Why do people continue do what they do when they know change is required? There are hundreds or thousands of questions why. The point is, if change is needed in one's life, then change must take place. The difficulty comes when self gets in the way.

Leaving the military resulted in many changes in my life. I had to adjust to a different way of living. The day I left the military for good was the beginning of a new life for my wife and myself. The things we both once enjoyed weren't there anymore for us to enjoy. Our lives were changed overnight. The enjoyment and convenience of shopping tax free at on-post facilities were gone after almost twenty-five years of having this privilege. Everything from food to clothes to gasoline could be purchased tax-free on base. Living on a military base gave us a sense of security from the outside world. Every major military installation has posted at its entry a military police who checked cars for proper registration and identification. No one got on base without proper identification.

I myself had to adjust to waking up one morning and not having the authority over large groups of personnel that I once had. The only person I had in my life to care for was my wife. I had to learn to talk in a softer tone of voice. Talking to my wife like I sometimes talked to my soldiers didn't go over too well. This is something I am still working on.

After I started another job everyday I had to quickly realize that someone else was in charge. It was hard for me to just sit back and watch some things take place before my eyes. It was, and still is, hard for me to be quiet when I know decisions don't rest with me. But one thing you can be sure of: I speak up if there is a cause. I do not let anyone take advantage of me or belittle the things I believe in.

It's been four years since I retired. I have not completely gotten over the shock, but as each day goes by I am getting better. I tell you this about myself to let you know that it is not all about you or me. We have other people in this world that we have to consider. No matter how long we have been accustomed to something there might come a day when change will be required. God did not create this universe just for you or I to live in alone. What we do and say along our journey will have an effect on others.

I realize that we all probably have at least one habit that we would like to get rid of. I sure do. When it comes to things that are damaging to my spiritual and physical well being, I make it a habit to stay as far away as possible. Sometimes the devil tries to sneak one in on me but God has given us a means of escape out of every temptation *(1 Corinthians 10:13)*. Self doesn't care about controlling habits or its spirit. Self will indulge in anything and everything that will make the flesh feel good. Because self tends to operate without a conscience, it doesn't necessarily care what others feel or think; its main goal is immediate satisfaction.

I was in a conversation with a man who had recently started on a physical fitness program. He told me that he didn't acknowledge his state of poor physical condition until one day he saw *himself* in a storefront window that he was walking by. He said that he was shocked by the way he looked. Until that moment he failed to realize why he didn't have the energy to play with his young son. This man was a physical therapist and knew the importance of taking care of one's body. He knew the importance of eating healthy foods, and exercising the body. The things he taught and preached to others he failed to do himself.

Acknowledgement is the first step to change. Then it is important that we act on what we know. Having knowledge of something without following through on it is deceiving one's self. A mirror or glass will only reveal what's on the outside. The Word of God reveals your heart to you in order to start the change from the inside out. Change has to take place on the inside of a person before it can show up on the outside *(James 1:22-25)*. If one refuses to acknowledge that there is something that needs to change, they will never take the necessary steps toward change.

I know of people who are chain-smokers. They smoke one cigarette after the other. They cough excessively all the time. But they will refuse to acknowledge that the coughing might be related to the cigarette smoking. I know of one man who is a heavy smoker that has been told by the doctor several times to quit smoking. Every time you ask him why doesn't he quit he will always give you the same answer – he is not ready yet. I wonder what will happen when he develops cancer, or some other disease from cigarette smoking. Will he look at the doctor or his family and say to them "I am not ready to have cancer"? Coming face-to-face with the real self is sometimes hard, but it is the first step to change. Until we see our selves the way that God sees us, we will remain the same.

We must sometimes be willing to change at the expense of ourselves but for the good of others. We must understand that we cannot change ourselves, but it is God that changes us. We first must submit to Him in order to begin the process.

> *"For I know that in me (that is, in my flesh,) dwelleth no good thing: for to* <u>*will*</u> *is present with me; but how to perform that which is good I find not."*

> *(Romans 7:18)*

> *"O wretched man that I am! Who shall deliver me from the body of this death?*

> *I thank God through Jesus Christ our Lord. So then with the mind I myself serve the law of God; but with the flesh the law of sin."*

> *(Romans 7:24-25)*

Self can't change because self won't receive correction. Life itself is full of corrections. Our parents correct us, family members correct us, our friends correct us, our spouse corrects us, our employer corrects us, our spiritual leaders correct us, and most of all we are corrected by the Word of God. A person that will refuse correction will not make it very far in this world.

> *"Correction is grievous unto him that forsakes the way: and he that hateth reproof shall die."*
>
> *(Proverbs 15:10)*

God can send correction through a person or through an event. But the best place one can find correction is from the Word of God.

> *"All scripture is given by inspiration of God, and is profitable for doctrine, for reproof, for correction, for instruction in righteousness."*
>
> *(2 Timothy 3:16)*

<u>NOTES</u>

CHAPTER THIRTEEN

Self Likes To Pretend

Self likes to put on a front. Self appear to be one thing but turns out to be something totally different. This is what selfish pride will do. Having pride in one's self is one thing, but having too much pride can cause a person to try and live a lifestyle that he is not capable of at the present time. People that are self indulgent will sometimes live a lifestyle that is appealing and approved by others. They will try to live their lives to satisfy others, but at the same time they will neglect their own family. People who pretend set a false appearance and representation toward others.

Trying to please others is a hard thing to do, especially people of the world. The world presents a picture of how a person should live but doesn't show how he should prepare himself for afterlife. Selfish people don't think about how their family members will feel when they pass from this life into another. It is selfish of anyone to neglect preparations for eternity.

Not taking the steps to make Jesus Christ the Lord and Savior of your life is selfish. It's selfish because you want to live your life the way that you choose. You live in such a way that when you die your family and friends worry about where you might spend eternity. I think this would be harder on them than the loss itself. But it is only a temporary loss for Christians. Christians who die in the Lord will be reunited at the return of Christ *(1Thessalonians 4:16-17)*.

I am not minimizing the loss of any life, especially if the person happens to be family or a close friend. I know the pain, void, and hurt of losing someone close to you. I lost a brother in 1995, my mother in 1996, another brother in 2004, and a sister in 2004. So I have experienced the pain alone with all the feeling of emptiness. But having the hope of knowing that they are in heaven is one less thing to run through my mind. If they lived their life as a Christian, when they died those left behind have the hope that they are in heaven. The Bible says that Jesus Christ is the hope of our salvation *(1 Timothy 1:1)*. We get that hope by trusting and believing that heaven is our home when we die. People whom only care about their present day living and take no action to secure their future are selfish. They will pretend to have it all together but are only putting on a front. They don't care about their soul and could care less about how others will be affected by it when they are gone.

When my mother passed away I felt sick in my spirit, body, and soul. God really taught me about death when she passed away. God told me that I must understand life in order to understand death. He said that He came to give us life and to live it to its fullest *(John 10:10)*. For the many years I knew my mother she lived her life to the fullest for Christ. When she passed away the Holy Spirit gave me the comfort and hope of her destiny based on the life she lived. I knew my mother was a Christian because she lived her life as a Christian. So it was not a question whether or not she was in heaven. But because of the void, pain, and emptiness that I was dealing with, the Holy Spirit took me and showed me where she was. He gave me comfort in my time of sorrow. In the Spirit I went to heaven where my mother was. I didn't see her but the Spirit made it clear to my spirit that she was there. My mother lived her funeral. Her funeral was a "Home Going Celebration" because she loved Jesus and lived for Him. Every day Christians and non-Christians are writing their own eulogy whether good or bad, heaven or hell.

It is a sad and sinful thing when family members have to lie on the obituary to say something worthy and edifying about that person's life. And then the minister gets up and tries to preach them into heaven. My mother's funeral was different. We didn't have to make up good things to say, nor did the minister have to try and preach her into heaven. She went to heaven as a choice of her own. And we all have to choose. Every day we are choosing heaven or hell. My mother taught her children to live for Jesus Christ. She wanted her children to have a knowing hope that when she died she was going to heaven. She chose not to live a life of selfishness, but a life for Christ. She did not pretend to be a Christian but she lived a Christian life. It would have been much harder on me if my mother had chosen to live any other way. But she chose to set an example for her children, grandchildren, and those around her. We are to set that same example. She lived a life of loving and helping others while she was here on this earth. She taught me so much about life. Even though she has been gone for nine years, the things I learned from her are still guiding me today. I believe it is the parent's responsibility to introduce their children to Christ.

What I am about to address is becoming more and more common among a lot of Christians as well as non-Christians families. This is something that is not talked about in your typical homes. But I believe that it should be discussed before hand. That is – not having enough life insurance or not having any at all. It may seem difficult or morbid to discuss, but everyone should prepare for death financially as well as spiritually. My parents weren't just concerned about their present day living but they also looked ahead. Mother and Dad knew there would come a day when they would have to leave this earthly living. They didn't want to leave behind the trouble of burying them, so they made preparation early in their marriage. Today a funeral costs over $6,000.00 and the cost is increasing every year. Family members don't need to be faced with the cost of putting their love one away. There are so many other things for them to focus on during that time.

When I was a child and still at home, I can remember every month when the insurance man came to the house to collect the monthly insurance policy payment. My parents were diligent in keeping the policy current. Sometimes they didn't have enough to pay the full payment that was due, but the insurance man would allow them to make a partial payment and pay the rest at a later date. By the grace of God they never got so far behind that the policy became inactive. I am sure they could have used the money for other things to support the family. My father farmed as a "share cropper" and didn't make much money at all. My mother worked in the fields helping my father with the crops. The money they used to pay the insurance premium each month could have been used to satisfy their own desires. But their minds weren't just on themselves but their children also. This was important to them and they felt it was important for their children. I thank my Mom and Dad for their unconditional love.

Pretending to yourself and to your family that you have sufficient insurance and you know you don't is selfish pride. Even if you purchased a life insurance policy five or ten years ago it may not be enough to satisfy your requirements today. We need to stop living selfishly and start thinking about the ones who will be left behind to bear the burden.

I believe that it's important that every grown person has a living will and a legal Power of Attorney. Your family needs to know how to handle the things you leave behind. You may say, "I don't have anything to leave behind so why should I have a living will." Even if you don't have anything to be divided among others, a living will can state the details of your final days on this earth. It is the last time you are able to choose for yourself. A living will is your last request before you are buried. This would save the family a lot of time and would take the guesswork out of the whole process. It will also minimize strife amongst family members. It wouldn't hurt to talk over the detail of your living will with certain family members. I know that conversations as these are not your normal family conversations. But it is too late to talk about them when someone passes away. Maybe its time for parents to talk to their adult children, and adult children talk to their parents, husbands talk to their wives, and wives talk to their husbands about these issues. Whether it's life insurance, long-term health insurance, or a will, it needs to be discussed. When you are gone you no longer have any input about your life, so stop the pretending, drop the selfish pride, and come clean with yourself about these issues. You have always wanted to be in control so here is your chance. And don't be so selfish that you don't want anyone to know where these documents and other important papers are located. And don't forget to make copies. Remember when you are gone it is hard to communicate this information to anyone. The image that we leave of ourselves on this earth after death can be devastating to others.

NOTES

CONCLUSION

Sometimes we don't know just how selfish we are until we are put into a situation where God can change our hearts. Sometimes the people that are closest to us, i.e., spouse, family members, and our closest friends get to experience the worst of our selfishness.

I remember watching a movie a few years ago titled *"Regarding Henry."* In the movie Harrison Ford stars as Henry Turner. Henry was a slick, ruthless, arrogant, prideful, corporate attorney who was willing to do anything to win a case. Henry was all about himself. Henry would withhold prudent information from a judge and jury just to win a case. He was a bully to his teenage daughter and put much fear in her heart. He even cheated on his wife with his female lawyer friend. Everyone that Henry came in contact with he treated cruelly, and disrespected. Henry was all about himself. Henry had no moral respect for anyone or anything. He didn't even take the time to sit down to eat with his own family. Henry was too busy doing his own thing. He was all into himself. Late one night Henry stepped out to a local mini-market to purchase a pack of cigarettes. He accidentally interrupts a burglar in the process of robbing the store and is shot twice by the robber. After being in a coma for some time he wakes up to discover that he has no memory of his past. He has to relearn everything from reading and walking, to tying his shoes. After a long stay in the hospital and much physical therapy, it's time for him to go home. Henry refuses to go. He doesn't remember his wife and daughter and doesn't want to live with them. As his memory slowly returns, he remembers some things about his house, and asks to go home. After returning home to his wife and daughter he discovers some secrets about how he really used to be before his accident. Henry gets his old job back at the law firm. He discovers that his wife was having an affair with his best friend. After he uncovers this shocking truth, he leaves his wife and goes to live in a hotel. His female lawyer associate confesses to him that they were having an affair before his accident. Of course Henry doesn't remember any of this. One day at his job he discovers the truth about information on a case he had won illegally before his accident. With this revealed information Henry is determined to make things right with the client's wife, and himself. He goes to her house and hands her proof that her husband had been wrongfully accused. Henry quits his job and returns back home to his family.

Henry, a contributor to this society, functioned as a man with no moral standards. He was a man that was focused only on himself. He would resort to unethical strategies to achieve his goal. An unfortunate incident changed everything about Henry. Henry must now find a way to fit back in where he once was, but this time with a different personality and change of heart.

Even though this movie is based on a secular setting, I believe it applies to real life and the present time. Being selfish can ruin one's life. Unfortunately most of the time we never have the opportunity to correct all the wrong we have done to others. We are all selfish to some degree. God commands us to be selfless and not selfish. If you are reading this and have wronged someone because of your selfish ways, you have a chance to come clean with that person. First, repent to God and ask Him to forgive you. Second, go to that person if possible and ask for forgiveness.

> *"And they that are Christ's have cruci-fied the flesh with the affections and lusts.*
>
> *If we live in the Spirit, let us also walk in the Spirit.*
>
> *Let us not be desirous of vain glory, provoking one another, envying one another."*
>
> *(Galatians 5:24-26)*

> *"Wherefore let him that thinketh he standeth take heed lest he fall."*
>
> *(1 Corinthians 10:12)*

I pray this book has been a blessing to you and has changed your life in a positive way.

In Jesus Name,
James E. Puckett

<u>NOTES</u>

NOTES

<u>NOTES</u>

NOTES

<u>NOTES</u>

<u>NOTES</u>

To contact James E. Puckett

Visit:
www.jamespuckettministries.netfirms.com

Please include your comments.

Additional copies of *Denying One's self In A Selfish World* are available from your local bookstore, or at www.bbotw.com

Or contact:

INFINITY PUBLISHING COMPANY
1094 New Dehaven St, Suite 100
West Conshohocken, PA 19428

www.infinitypublishing.com
Toll-free (877) BUY BOOK (289-2665)

Previous books by
James E. Puckett

Living Life With Faith In God

*Keeping Your Mind Renewed In Your Spiritual Walk
With Christ*

Separation of Christian And Church

Fighting Fear With Faith

About The Author

JAMES PUCKETT is called to preach and teach the Word of God through evangelism. He was inspired by God in 1999 to spread the gospel through writing. He is the author of a number of books, including *Keeping Your Mind Renewed In Your Spiritual Walk With Christ*, and *Fighting Fear With Faith*. James is a retired Chief Warrant Officer from the United States Army with nearly twenty five years of active duty service. He resides in Knoxville, Tennessee, with his wife Brenda. James holds a Bachelor of Biblical Studies from Omega Bible Institute and Seminary. He states that the biggest problem we have as people is *self*.